Seventh Edition

Copyright © Anthony Anaxagorou 2014
First published 2012 *by* Out-Spoken Press

Design & Art Direction
Ben Lee

Printed & Bound by Print Resource

A Difficult
Place To
Be Human

For my Mother & Father

Most of the poetry I write is not for those with a Masters in Fine Arts or Literature. It's not even for other poets or publishers. It's for the guy driving the bus, the boy being bullied, the single mother carrying home her shopping, the son who wonders what his father's voice would sound like cheering from the sideline and the daughter who won't ever be noticed by anyone. It's for the invisible, the powerless and the lost. It's for people like me.

Contents

Some poetry only works on the
brokenhearted

From

remembrance

Football
Results

As a boy my father took silence over talk;
he would sit
deep inside his glasses
as if admiring their stillness
as I stayed picking myself out
from inside a draft.

Cigarette smoke made curtains
over Saturday afternoon's football results
his thin fingers rummaging
through that tawny beard
as if searching
for the good luck he'd lost
to the abrupt knock of his journey.

Absently
he would walk me to wherever,
our footsteps chipping away at the grey silence
as if the irritating wind
and then playful rain
marred those beloved glasses of his.

I can still hear those football results
I can still hear those Saturday afternoons

when I held his hand just to listen to him curse
the childish season that only wished to be felt.

My
Father's
Walk

I shake your hand now
our fingers match

we hug
with men between us
speaking concisely
on politics
your silence
still breaking the bones of my points
with eyes too similar to ever meet
so soon until your hurtling rage
floods forward to drown the water
I drink
hurling us back
with our conversation
half spelt
inside the same torn kitchen
I raised my first words in
when your face reminded me
of a fatherless little boy
and your thinning footsteps were all I had
to look up to.

Broken
Shells

The truth is a single egg
wishing quietly for a voice
somewhere from within the womb of its time
it waits to be born,
to sing up into the ages as a folk song
that people will recall and say
'yes I know this, I remember this,'
but music is a harmony between silence and love
and courage is the only act which can unlock freedom
opening a new growth, an unfettered gala of true spring
reaching out across classrooms and newspaper sheets
and the auto-cue of straight-eyed anchormen
as every enemy infected by hate
stops to watch the sun
buy back the sky with all its gold!
Yes friends the truth is a single egg
complete as the last word placed at the end of the longest poem
it's there, as a mother is, as a mountain is,
and from its permanence it watches us only to weep
us who fight, who thrust our wickedness into the core of days,
us who invent death, destroying the fleece of our world
so we can build dust on top of dust, superfluous graves hanging,
forgotten cemeteries that lean into unrest and the truth
buried beneath it all.

In the resplendent colours of a dream
it clings onto the imagination for life
pulling against the scrawl of some midnight scholar
who writes maniacally I won't forget you,
you didn't happen just to die.
So the truth becomes a dream
swimming within the cognisance
of scholarship and poetry
wandering as an orphan amidst the blur of the true
and the untrue

A Difficult Place To Be Human

the opposition vs. the motion
the information against the misinformation
because the truth is a single egg
and a lie is a million sperm
racing to undo it
beating against its weathered shell
with ego, deceit and corruption
until it can no longer withstand the onslaught
and a lie eventually permeates the truth.

A young boy came and sat beside me
on an old bench where I was writing this.
Peering over into my notebook he said,
'your handwriting is similar to mine.'
'Really? Well I'm writing a poem about the truth' I said
he laughed like good luck with that
'I would help you but I don't know much about the truth.'
'Well that's a lie' I said, 'here…finish it.'
'You serious?'
'Yes.'
'Ok.'

When I come home and my mum says she missed me
or my best mate whose dad beats him for no good reason says,
'dude, on your next birthday can we blow out the candles together?'
Or
when I step off an aeroplane and my granddad ruffles my hair
kissing my forehead at the airport
or I brush past Stephanie from the year above
letting her sweet smell pin me to the floor
I reckon truth has something to do with that.
And when I'm scared, like really scared, scared to even open my eyes
I think of all those kids who'll never open their eyes again
and I soar high for them all.

Still, the one thing about truth that really gets me
is when Sundays come my mum she boils me an egg
putting it in front of me she says,
'you'll need to be patient with how you approach this
delicate with how you open this
because its contents is soft and sensitive
some can handle it
others ruin it before they get a chance to know what it is
but you, you will know how to treat this egg.'

Handing the book back to me
I ask out of interest, 'why the egg thing?'
Biting on his nails he says,
'you know I think my mum uses that
because she used to love a guy who always said
that the truth is a single egg
and a lie is a million sperm
I guess she was right
because I've never met him.'

Glasses

I always spoke to your glasses
the heavily tinted ones, taciturn and stoic.

I had so many questions for your mind and mouth
but instead you just turned your glasses on me

so now I see
all I need to see
without the annoyance of glasses.

Dying
Man

We feel it all, everything
besides death.

It comes with quiet appraisal
dressed as wind, as minute or weekend
asking life to grow once again
in its garden of bodiless weather.
Bones beg the mercy of muscles
but the body knows the direction
of its next journey
remaining as silent as flesh.

They all came closer in to see
the sight of a dying man
filling the halls with wonder
and despair for this frail and tired thing.
Some turned to prayer whilst others
watched through a trembling lens
forgiving their life for its petty troubles
in an instant where rain dominated the earth.

His breath studied the heavy clock,
his eyes nodding at the life spilling
over in others until
nothing else remained to be watched
the doors had closed, the people had left
and the windows had gone blind;
packing his soul away he took the finishing step
into that radical subterranean night of his highest glory.

Last
Question

I watched from a safe place

the grand hearse mowing against its finality
the surrounding congregation fixing
their useless reflection
strict on its metallic roll.

Inside myself I asked him
'so what's it like old man
is it anything to write home about?'

The hearse dragging towards the end
at its own sad silent speed

with the fumes suffocating the God
trapped in all our shallow wounds
my question had finally gone
to find its answer.

Tell Me About Love

Friend

We'd seen each other in the ugliest forms
fighting, broken-nosed, laughing with bloody gums and torn skin.
We'd seen each other heartbroken, drunk somewhere,
gripping the neck of a bottle
as if it were our own suicidal fault.
I had seen him asleep, assured that nobody could ever hurt him
alive in his dream
positive that a nightmare could be shaken off
or that a good thought could be prolonged
just to be remembered until tomorrow.
        He had seen me topless, skinny,
saying he wished ribs were stronger,
that he wished he could trust them but he couldn't
           neither could I.

Years later we were sitting with the many who were like us
in a crackled yard
where the smell of sweat was always the same
and the noise was always an industry of chainsaws.
He had returned from disappearing again looking different
when he drank
his eyes would fall over more frequently
like he was trying to leave himself in a place of hopeless sobriety.
        He spoke with paving slabs
muscled to his tongue, each word I would chase down
some old hawkish street
        just as I did before.

In a time that favored the shape of days
we spoke about the way of the world
its calamity, its misfortune and all those unsponsored
backs we once knew.
There were never questions as long as answers
had a sound, there was brilliance in his eyes,
stardom in his drunkenness,

A Difficult Place To Be Human

I could see again the genius I called friend
up until I asked him for his thoughts on Love
- its unflowering wreckage, abandonment and thin gamble.
            Chucking the last pool of liquor to the back of his throat
he bowed the glass and walked clear out the place
            leaving nothing but me behind.

Now I sit hurting some struggles later somewhere unknown to him
in an age of untempered concerns, worries of a different texture.
Wars still occur - he was right about that,
books are forever weapons - he was right about that too,
but I miss his happening troubles, those chattering chipped teeth
that spoke in a universal currency
yet just the other day a note arrived
addressed to the younger me, a me only he still had,
it was hand written, defiant in the age of model binary.
            It read plainly as if it had discovered for itself
the shortest response to my most lasting concern
            forgive it all.

Talent

The old lady who lost her old man
sat with me on the park memorial bench -
the one with the rusted
In Loving Memory plaque.

She would turn a patient ring around
her forth finger in the same soft way
she would tune her radio in
to listen to her afternoon stories.

I would hold in my hand some heavy book
that she'd already lived

and after a chapter of silence she told me
that soon she would die. That she's
not afraid. That she knows people
far more fearful who did it exceptionally well.

'Then that is a kind of talent,' I remarked
to the live side of her face
where the waning beams of October sunlight
fought hard to protect.

'Talent my dear is not found in fearless dying
talent is in surviving to die.'

Lose
My
Voice

I could lose my voice to you
in a crushing heartbeat on a stale hospital bed
with plastic veins trembling inside those parts of me
that you would once sink into
to try and find an unresolved part of yourself.
In a flurry of pale words I might sound like a prayer
being led to the end of the world's last bible
only to find that those final few pages were missing
and that God was just a quiet bit of white space
sitting with everything that's ever been said
and everything that's ever been lost.

My fading eyes might resemble those unplugged stars
that would once nourish your world with a light
I would kindle from the beams of an old love,
the same light that once upon a youth came between our kisses
the kind that the moon would try to get between
so as to place itself inside a moment of tenderness
for it knows somehow that the battle against its stony night
is infinite.

We created a family of memories you and I
the incubating sheets of each year
joining to form a calendar filled with Andrew's first steps
and Stella's first dance, those baby words that must feel like
the voice of one dead
coming back to touch the heart of his beloved for the last time
our children are complete islands
that persuade that moment when the soul abandons itself
in a burning cathedral to rise up and breathe again
the cool sun of life.

A Difficult Place To Be Human

Close yourself to this deflated loaf and just feel my words
because my mouth has been defeated of its only use
and my body has at last forgotten itself,
the strength it once lifted
the miles it so easily trampled on
have now all surrounded me in a reckless grope
fragility, is a confine that I pray you never know,
it's an open cell free of its lock,
it's an imagination being held hostage by a broken wheelchair,
it's watching everything grow wild
whilst you're forced to shrink further into yourself
but love, love is an indefatigable celebration
the only hand that can never fold because right now
in this hospital room
amongst these hanging wires and this air that tortures
my heavy lungs
love is the only medicine I have.
So come close
and put your hands inside mine
so I can hold again the long fingers of tomorrow;
my skin runs ashamed by the breath that keeps all this poison
for itself
so take from me all the words you'll need to write the poem
that if death is to style my little future
I know will follow.

I could lose my voice to you
if you could somehow lose your death to me,
let me take you from that room where unconvinced flowers
bow in their vase
as if they too had peered into my heart and become stricken
by its long lament
and in return you could take from me this voice,
these words and this gift

that now sound like a promise losing faith in its deepest conviction
but if I had known
that your last few words would have sounded like they did
and your body would have convulsed and stiffened
as white coats came rushing past me
then maybe I could have thought of something
more beautiful to say,
maybe I could have read you the poem I was writing
whilst you slept under a stuttering beep
that allowed life to meet you through a thinning tube and maybe,
just maybe,
we could have shared that last bit of white space together
but instead, all I could do was drown in the storm you gave my eyes
throwing myself into the arms of a doctor
who repeated the word brave without even looking at me
then gave me a card with a number I should call
if things ever got too much.

Your room is clean now my love
no more machines, no more encouraging smiles,
no more waiting flowers;

by tomorrow no doubt there will be another loved one
fighting her last battle against the precious air,
and there will be more husbands, more sons and more daughters
who'll write poems under a stuttering beep
because they don't know any other way of coming to terms
with the tragedy of life's final act

I just hope that they reach the end in peace
because you were the poem I couldn't save
and this was the voice I couldn't lose.

When the
circus is full
of clowns

nobody stops
to think about
the Lion.

All I Can
Say Is

I was here

I was there

To those places that hold freedom
by its first promise I have been

into the natty forests that shiver
as the lashes of the world
I have gazed
into those soundless dunes
those bloodless lagoons kissed
hard by a stanza of mosquitos
raging with a hundred sharp lips
I have swum
laying awake on an unborn beach
the moon awaiting the return
of its perfect moth, tomorrow's sun
distantly dreaming of its holy eagle
I have been

among the poorer markets
to find communes of fruit endless in figure
hounded by starving language
decorating each gradient of corner
painting music with yellow tone
speaking to me in blunt teeth
-the imagination of sound -
and poverty, poverty, so much poverty
the stricken countenance
inwrought on the faces that know only
corn, rice and bread,
hands extending down into the still earth
praying to retrieve a pardon
for the spine of a dying peasant
who stands
like a prized border strained by war.

I have buckled under the world's racism
which spins human blood
into a raped rainbow of dead colors.
Go feel the hammer-pulse of oppression
then put your sweet life on it!
Find God in a clever church
that toys with comfortable dreams
helping gruel sink to its mellow stomach;
from the bowels of disparity
the blue-bottles feast relentlessly
off their victim's bleating misery
so know I have seen it, our earth's
failed suicide note

and to where it ends I can never go
all I can say is I was here, I was there,

in both the familiar and strange rains
for the melting of snow back into stone
with my hammer and nails
working for those unrested
men and women who rise
from the unmapped quarters
to take my hand and call me brother,
showing me a family in the shacks,
a love in the destitute sinking apologies
of every place I go to
in the hope of flying
the punctured banner of humankind.

On Exit

What is hell but another rich city?
Each way begs to enter
but the only exit belongs to the muddy ground,
billboards tell you everything you will never need to know
and oversexed girls make mountains look young,
the rush sweeps tying lives together
as the machine prowls our dreams
filling them with immortal batteries.
It's hard on the eyes
a carnival of pregnant sorrow
the consumer is the consumed
as the poets pen moves to dead-drum rhythms,
sour tunnels of light turning to melt over graffiti walls,
we're all stuck in a London signature
living with these hyper sirens in a culture that yells
take but never return.
See how the sky looks down on us,
the earth jolts with cocaine at its feet
its skeleton a branded rifle,
its pedagogue bleeding ideas into the future's ill frame
humanity a concept debatable.

For once give me the news without the lies
so as to leave each page lost for words,
each caption a saintly blank,
show me a revolution that doesn't end on a Sunday
and start again next Saturday.
Where is he that will save the life
of a child different from his?
Can socialism exist without the champagne?
There are babies with crayon hearts
making weapons from weeping flowers,
there are babies that will be dead
by the time this poem ends

A Difficult Place To Be Human

because every struggle is a repeating sentence
that murdered its full stop.
I would pray but heaven blew itself up in its last war,
I would fight but the real enemy is never seen,
turn away from these towers and fumes
from this years rhetoric
and leave it all to dance inside its flame.
All things make rust eventually
as the tender good die unwritten
so long
these are the last days
as never before has there been a more violent group
of man
the flags are all wounded,
the borders lay spineless
leaving the greatest famine to exist
inside the disaster of corrupt hearts.

Love me beyond an ending

                                                                     she told me

I was kicking stones in my head again

                                                                     she told me

I bring the distance too close
so take me to where fairytales are woven on beaches
where waves can die happy in the sand
and your pen doesn't move anymore.
Take me to where I can see it all
from the eyes of a genius,
from the eyes of a child,
and on exit leave the world to make trophies from its despair

so close the door
because here you're safe
here the writing sleeps.

On
That
Day

and they managed to save
the little girl from drowning
by giving back her boat

and the shepherd from
the Middle East could live again
when they finally released his hills

and the fishermen from the South
cast their nets so far out into the ocean
that the moon seemed to bend closer

and the taxi drivers
played loud the first song they heard
after kissing the mouths of their wives

and the boy who went to war
returned home for the comfort of his mother's soup
and the dreams he would have in his own bed

and the girl who was raped by a soldier
rinsed her breasts with tears
watching how the drain swallowed him at last

and the coltan miners
were handed mobile phones
to call their children and scream proud their love

and the poets
could only write about the things pure
and unaffected
and the borders touched hands
and the miners were shown light
and the guns were fed to water
and the books were returned

and the flags felt ashamed
and the fruit tasted real
and the cattle were left to run
and the prisons all melted
and the forests stretched

and the politicians
and the generals
and the bankers
and the owners
and the editors
and the monarchy
and the liars
and the bankers
and the politicians
and the murders

all understood the nature of dying

and so the street vendors
bellowed the news
that Capitalism had at last gone home.

Two
Syllables

Six
Letters

Two syllables
six letters
nailed to the sea.

An island at ease
with the cool definite running of waves,
I climb through the smell of its thirsty earth,
its lazy olive trees and lost monasteries
that beguile an unsatisfied God.

Trek deeper, past the cologne of orange groves,
the hacked meats and leaking salads
where a constellation of bruised rocks hurt for its history
and there you'll find it all weighing on the back
of some old donkey forgotten in its dystrophy.

A donkey who took the strain of injustice,
whose hooves quietly bled while
the morally good gripped the hand of every struggle
but his. While the liberals and philanthropists
helped move every preposterous volcano,
loaded with effort to block the liquid stampede of empire,
of colonialism and genocide, but our dear donkey,
the one who dreamt of a simple clean moon
became too familiar with blood - his journey laden
with misfortune but still
he went on.

United with his brothers
united with his sisters
even when the winter rains ceased to dampen
the heart of the Levant,
the summer sun ceased to shine and started
instead to burn
and the autumnal wind carried within it the puked stench
of a gutted village,
still he went on.

Around he saw his island's scabbed pyrite
exposed like the earth's very own entrails.
Wine dripped from wooden tables.
Blood dripped from wooden tables
and everywhere was ending.
But that was then
in a time when donkeys were slaughtered
for their grieving,
when the pestilence came to test our beaches,
our pride and character.
In a time they would rather have us forget
but way down in our villages, estranged and plain
there were a few

who fought to restore what once was
who craved peace
who sang loud the song in their hearts
that of an island

two syllables
six letters
nailed to the sea.

Old
Palestine

Old Palestine is on fire:

From a distance
it smolders at the knees
fading with a dark flint
into a memory of holes, of gaps
of inertia.

We know Palestine
but we do not know Palestine.

Cemeteries know Palestine,
ones where bent mothers
howl into the earth like
God has always been a little boy
sleeping underground.

Bullets know Palestine,
charged thieves that spark to wreck
a shepherd's simple dream,
a mother's garden pride,
a father's living-room chair.

Rubble knows Palestine,
homes where village windows
lament their shattered vision
and exploded bricks lay in a cluster
over unburied bodies.

Soldiers know Palestine,
ruthless sharks that boast
with the apparatus of carnage,
gutless misanthropes, racists
of dead skin.

Injustice knows Palestine,
trails of refugees swelling up the red soil
like borders where instruments come to bury
their last songs, prayers question their palms
and yes

grief knows Palestine
pushing it back to the temperature that burns
everything but the pale tyrant
everything but the sea
everything but repetition

and the Congo knows Palestine,
Sierra Leone knows Palestine,
Afghanistan knows Palestine,
Iraq knows Palestine,
Haiti knows Palestine,

but we do not, we choose instead
to turn away, to forfeit those ancient roses
for the damp simplicity of a million weeds
because without truly knowing
there can be nothing to remember.

Jamaican

Could the following boys please remain seated:-

Kabir Hussain
Omar Ahmed
Cong Tang
Ibrahim Nawaz
Pablo Martinez
Taha Wasim
Viktor Flyorov
Ade Uwagbo
Nabil Mohammed
Anton Nikoli
Feng Wu
Atash Rezaei
Christopher White
Andreas Christophi
and
Efran Brackman

A Difficult Place To Be Human

The Master's Revenge

There will be revenge
but it will be different from yours
it won't involve blood or murder
or deception
it won't turn sophisticated people to rubble
then call them underdeveloped, primitive and backwards
it won't need military budgets,
fear, prejudice or gender oppression
it will be simple, uncomfortable
and absolute
it will present itself calmly
there will be no screams
there will be no protests
just this:

You are the owner of all energy
needed to destroy or create worlds
within you lies the peace of Akhenaton
the vision of Imhotep
we can go further
the first messiah
you are the writer of knowledge
the keeper of truth
it's looking at you through the stones
in the history of the mountains
and the DNA of the earth
you're there
this wicked narrative is new
it's evil and unwell
1000 years ago you were teaching them
they were lost, barbaric, never knowing
the evolution of language
of culture the influence you had
you still have, you must have
because you're far from dead

listen
to the speakers, the knowers,
the ones who tell you to open pages
and find yourself there
reinvent the past
pay the oppressor little mind
little mind fear genius
because it knows your story
it knows about the Old Kingdom
and the middle periods
from Moorish Spain to Muslim medicine
it knows about African mathematicians
and the stone calendar circles of Nabta Playa
it knows, that's why it denies
that's why it tells you to kill yourself
death has many faces
if something is made ill
why swallow it?
Don't accept it, renounce it and go back
to before the chattel
the division and genocide
before the White Jesus,
before the Crusades
and the foreign religions that came with priests
and swords
discover the hidden world
because history is self-serving
self-fulfilling look in the prisons
look in the armies,
look in the places filled with the broken,
the destitute, the trampled on
the us but not them
look and see
what happens when you
become apathetic

when revenge is just for radicals
when you believe the story
they tell you
when your only weapon is a gun,
when your only hope is a fantasy,
when your knowledge is obsolete,
when your woman is a bitch,
when your brother is a threat,
and your oppressor is your master,
your standard, your ideal
don't ask for mercy
it won't be given
lock it off, leave it there,
it's dead it's done
the damage consecrated the sickness
it doesn't work
so start again
with just this:

When they ask you for a beginning teach them
about the Grimaldi
about Menes and the first dynasty
when they ask you about women
speak to them of Isis, Hatshepsut and Cleopatra
when they ask you about European languages
refer them to Coptic and Western Semitic
tongues, explain how 50% of the Greek lexicon
is comprised of a Non-Indo European language
give examples
when they ridicule you for saying init
claiming the word as being
Jamaican Patois let them know that it's
a contraction of isn't it, which is a contraction
of is it not, which is English and not Patois is it not?

When they ask you about war and peace
inform them that the word war comes from the
Old English wyrre meaning to bring into confusion
mention the Golden Age of Egypt,
communicate the fact that civilizations
which have experienced the greatest periods of peace
have been matriarchal - say that twice.
Include the fact that 70% of Native Americans
did not ever wage war with each other, refer them to
Conquest: Sexual Violence and American Indian Genocide
by Andrea Smith
keep close to mind the Haitian revolution,
Toussaint L'ouverture and Dessaline
if they interject calling you Afrocentric or a conspiracy theorist
reply with these names:-
Volny, Gerald Massy, Martin Bernal, Bouavl and Brophy
continue
discuss human nature, how we remain
products of our environment, how we mirror what we see,
how certain genes are activated or deactivated
in our childhood
determining who we become later,
explain what you mean by White Supremacy
as a political tool to divide and undermine those
who don't fit the aesthetic
discuss Thomas Spence and
the making of the English working class
look at denigrate families in the US and Anthony Stokes
speak of Palestine with courage
declare that before the 15th May 1948 Zionists had already
expelled 250,000 Palestinians
emphasize that people are not born bad
that before capitalism and feudalism communalism
was how we lived
not primitive but equal.

Do not negate your woman. There is more to feminism
than her physical appearance, you may wish to talk about
Simone De Beauvoir, Bell Hooks and Angela Davis
then poetry, the spoken word that predates the written word
oral tradition, art and storytelling.
Speak until the sun has risen and set a thousand times
wear the crown that doesn't need a stolen jewel to shine,
assure them that you are made from love
that you speak from love because that is from where
you were born
play them a song, read them a haiku
teach them how to dance

many will laugh at you
many will brand you insane
yet when has madness ever really mattered here?
Some will listen, some will stay
and you will grow into friends,
into solidarity, into the forever
we dream about
so treasure your woman
treasure your man
because we're all we have

peace is the master's revenge

so stand in the present, draw for the future
and shoot with all the ammunition of the past.

Dialectics

I'm talking about the young brothers
bunched together
under broken street lights
walking backwards into shadows
because for some
shadows are safer than cells.
Young brothers
that don't believe knowledge will pay
like the grams they keep close
to their side with the stripes
on their tracksuit bottoms that balloon over those skinny legs
forced to carry society's failures
brothers that learnt to hate
before they learnt to say their fathers name,
adopting a killer's pose to try and conceal
everything they've been through
from windows to hospital wards
to meat-wagons to watch if I see him again
young brothers
who prey on young sisters
whose faces are far too beautiful for these unnatural streets
sisters who just want to play
but grow up knowing what a blow job is
and what an abortion entails
and what crack smells like
and the precise angle that a head should be tilted at
in order to stop a broken nose from bleeding
sisters who only ever wanted to love their brothers
who envied Cinderella not because she found her prince
but because her's was a story they had to read alone.

I'm wondering about the abusers
who sit in decaying rooms
with dead bodies that hang for curtains
blocking out the arms of the day

as rotten eyes chase a tail of smoke
in some poor attempt to defeat reality,
where depression comes in crisp shopping bags
or stiff price tags
and graffiti scarred lifts that refuse to leave the ground
where windows in their uniform
all appear to be bleeding with rain,
I'm thinking about the writers
who stay awake talking to their suffering
in a private notepad the colour of God
while the tall and healthy sleep inside visions of grandeur
and the tabloid print machines spit out tomorrow's
foreign enemies
he writes to the pulse of a dying heart
in a cryptic tongue
that teachers will later call unintelligent and undesirable
but his friends all get it
as they take his words and shoot them to the sky
until the night our young writer
tried to save a sister
from getting her nose broken by an over zealous boyfriend
sirens chopping up the limbs of night
the story writes itself from here on
because justice can only be justified by the most unjust
so he received 18 months for resisting arrest.

I'm howling about the system that denies people their history
and teaches racism in all the correct places
that hetropatriachal menace that strips women
of their natural cloth
giving them instead a perverted flashlight
to blind themselves with,
I'm beating my fists against Capitalism
for the slum dwellers from the heavy skies of Mumbai
to Cape Town

A Difficult Place To Be Human

from the paradise lost in Chagos and back round to Rio
it's all blood for gold, blood for coltan, blood for diamonds
and blood for oil
blood, the only resource expendable
where poverty's a man-made condition
and slavery doesn't need chains and whips to function
and just because people aren't hanging anymore
doesn't mean the idea of White Supremacy
was buried with Willy Lynch and George Washington
there is silent murder in these supposed times of equality.

I'm writing about the broken hearted
the ones whose life has turned in on them
who have only ever known loss
because they couldn't pay bills and her idea of love
was sold to her by a magazine dressed in bright chandeliers,
to the ones who eat alone in a room made of memories
because they weren't afraid to say I Love You
but on occasions love dies before it's born.
Yes I'm speaking about the elderly
who've come full circle to be reacquainted with infancy
the ones who need a steady hand, a clear pair of eyes
or warmth they can afford. So in the end
I'm left talking about the artists
the ones who salvage the human spirit
who on some days don't want to write, or sing
or act, or paint or dance
who want to leave their suffering alone for a moment
just to imagine what birds must feel like
when the summer opens up the gates to its sky,
to give their skin to the body of a quiet stream
or maybe just to hold the hand of a stranger
but that's only on some days
because on most days the world beats art into us and
it's always the brave few who go on to save a billion desperate lives.

A Difficult Place To Be Human

If I
Told
You

What if I told you that all life is African?

What if I told you that the oldest human culture developed in Katanga Congo

or what if I told you that the Ethiopian Australopithecus known as Lucy is also known as Dinquinesh?

What if I told you that every Black face is the descendent of an Ancient Egyptian or that no country has as many pyramids as Sudan?

What if I spoke about the library in Kemet and Alexander's pillaging of knowledge, the burning of books, of culture and philosophy?

What if I told you that the Vikings were the most pre-eminent slave owners and that the 11th century saw Dublin as the slave capital of the world?

Would you believe me if I told you that White people enslaved their own kind first or that St. Patrick was a run-away slave – a drapetomaniac?

What If I told you that Pythagoras was taught by some smooth faced Egyptians, as was Thales and Anaxamander?
What if I explained Egyptian Mystery Schools to you?

What if I told you all great European philosophers were trained by Black Africans in Ionia or what if I told you what Herodotus said about the Colchians?

What if I told you what Ghandi said about Western Civilisation?
What if I told you about Europe's dark ages and how they sat in comparison to the empires of Mali and Kush?

A Difficult Place To Be Human

What if you knew about Abubakari II?

What if I told you that Columbus never stepped foot on American soil and that Africans were navigating the globe with papyrus-reed ships in 2600BC?

What if you knew about Cheop boats and that Europeans didn't have a concept for latitude or longitude until the 18th century?

What if I told you that racism was invented?

What if I told you that we only ever oppress those who are powerful?

What if I told you that in the 16th and 17th century White indentured servants and Black slaves fought subjugation together?

What if I told you about J.F. Blumenbach and his obsession with racial purity and White slave women?

What if you knew about David Walker's Appeal?

What if I told you what Columbus said when he first saw Arawak Indians in the Bahamas?

What if I told you about the suggestion made by priest Bartolomé de Las Casas then what if I told you how many lives were lost to the grin that swept across Columbus's face?

What if I told you that nothing has really changed and that racism is ever present?

What if I told you about that battle at Wounded Knee in 1890 and the massacre of 300 Native Americans with the Hotchkiss gun?

What if I told you that Native American's today have a life expectancy of 46?

What if I told you that the enemy is White Supremacy?

What if I didn't care about African history, or the genocide
of indigenous people and instead wrote poems about
Winston Churchill, Thomas Jefferson and Abraham Lincoln
and I refrained from talking about the 54 countries that make
up the British commonwealth?

What if I told you that the abolition of slavery had nothing
to do with philanthropy but pure economics?

What if I told you religion has killed more people than it's
saved and that nothing can buy you peace?

What if I told you that a teacher's job is to help you understand
what you already know?

What if I told you about freedom, what if I promoted violence
instead of self-reliance?
What if I said everyone that looked like you was a killer,
a bomber, a terrorist?

What if I told you that the media lies, that the news is censored
and that everything has an agenda?

What if I told you about Miltion Friedman
and the Chicago School of Economics?
What if I told you about Neoliberalism?

What if I told you about Edward Bernays or that since the
invasion of Iraq 110,721 innocent civilians have died nameless?

What if I told you about the systematic imprisonment of
Black and Latino males in America?
What if you knew the worth of every prison inmate?

What if I told you about Francis Galton and the
Eugenics Movement?

What if I told you about NSSM 200?

And what if I quoted Emerson or Thoreau and I worked
on a building site or I knew that Shakespeare
invented over 1700 words including the word assassination?

What if I was reading The Apology on the bus ride to work
and work happened to be cleaning office toilets?

What if I was ugly but knew how to make her smile?

What if I told you that music is not popular but universal
intelligent noise resonating from the soul of the universe?
What if I told you that in every bit of me is every bit of you?

What if I stopped writing for a second, or a week or a year would I
miss something?

What if I told you that love is forgiveness breathing and every man
wants to be held as tightly as every woman does?

What if I told you that we all want to be wanted
and that cruelty is how weak men respond to fear?

What if I told you that the hardest man I'd ever known
loved me the most?

What if I told you the first time I punched someone I felt strong
but the crying that I did that night introduced me to a weakness
I'd never felt before?

What if I told you the first time I kissed a girl an earthquake
found my legs and each time I get my heart broken
I become a better poet?

What if I told you that a single act of genius is the result of a
thousand failures and that every master knew nothing at the start?

What if I told you I believe in you, in your heart and your life?
What if I told you the greatest gift I ever received was being told
I can?

What if I told you that you wrote this?

Now

what if I never told you?

Some poetry
only works

on the broken
hearted

Waiting

I will love you from that home in me
that has always stayed waiting

that home in me that has always
stayed waiting for staying.

For You, Dear Friend

This is for you dear friend
trapped in a secret you can't bear to tell
fighting the darkness for a moment of peace
sleepless in your troubles
your drowning depression
as your insides look for a way out,
and the sharp horn pressed coldly
against your hope cries into a silence
only death understands;

I know what it's like
to wash your face and still feel dirty
I know what it's like
to be loved and still feel hated
I know what it's like
to be alone
to see the flames within your own
self doubt your own self
berate your own self
I came close, to the closest part
of an ending but I grew to love
the beginnings that fall at the feet
of every failure
I thought back,
on all the yesterdays I had collapsed
only to see that today was only possible
because I refused to stay down,
I refused to be the mud, that part of the earth
people walk all over
I let it go, I watched it leave and I kissed
you on the lips because you said
you hadn't felt anything in years,
and we put on a song to dance to
until our bodies were so full of music

that we went to sleep that night in a melody
no instrument could catch,
and you slept in the sky of my arms
dreaming of eagles, infinity and sunshine.

I will never know what it feels like
to cry like you,
I will never know what it's like
to be Black, to be a woman,
to be poor and told your whole life
things that make you compose a list
of a million ways to kill yourself.

I won't always be there when the eagle
puts on its boots and comes to seek you out
or when you slam every door or your friends
don't answer the phone and your mum's left you in tears again.

No I can't always be there
when the beauty that is your face
turns into something unrecognizable,
something far from here,
something that spells words in a thin trail
of melting mascara running down your cheeks
you whisper a goodbye
but when you come close to the closest
part of an ending
think of yourself smiling and see the child
throwing bread to the ducks,
see the child opening her presents on Christmas day,
winning an award, learning to swim, saying the words
I love you and saying them again.

See the child that has done nothing wrong,
that wants to dance and laugh and sing,
see it all as it once was
pure, still, perfect

and keep whatever calm you find
for me because when I come in crashing
reeking of mud and covered in the earth's shoe prints
I'm going to need your heart.

Can you do that for me?
And all I ask from you
is that you keep it together
because you're harder to pick up

when you're in pieces.

A Difficult Place To Be Human

In

side

She didn't like being touched.
She made that clear from the start.
He said there are a million ways
to go inside.

I've heard that before.

He played her poems,
read her music
the kind he had written on a night
when insects rioted in his mouth,
on the thick terror of anorexic hope
he jabbed out those words using the marrow
of every catastrophe he had fallen beneath

to which her body thawed
and her eyes broke apart
undoing their beautiful
white storm.

Fist

You can't breathe from inside a fist;
wolves patrol wounds
the night launches itself into you
everything with a root quivers
opening honestly
over a dreamless vista, a dead window
where nothing speaks, or holds or loves,
thoughts implode
and clarity is a lonely lover
muttering mad hymns into the cyclic rope
of suicide.

Outside fortunate crowds
move towards a foreign sign,
the rushed course of the future
happens
so it can repeat,
that singular moment of success, sex,
triumph shared with nude palm trees
as strong alcohol flirts with coal diamonds,
beaches married to beaches
names remembered only by cheap lives
and famished minds,
short death celebrating the victory of long life
-ridiculing the poverty of earth-
the oracle spreading itself
beautifully under a divorced sky

and all I can do is watch
having walked upon a life
littered with shivers of dark glass

I've nothing in my hopes
because it's all in my fist
punishing me into another day.

I Mean

It wasn't always like this
I mean
I didn't have to be the man
to be the man in a world that loses touch
with its fingers just so it can boast about having bigger hands
I mean

there was a time where you could hold me
and not be conscious about the size of my muscles
or the speed of my car or how well I could fight
but rather your concern was with how long I'd lay beside you
just to tell you things my mouth
was still trying to learn the language to
because just having you there
whilst the rain gave its silver sheen to all things dry
and the couple upstairs
were still afraid to understand one another
when your skin kissed mine in a dark room
held together by candles illuminating the worry
that made my eyes look rich and I would stare
with too much hair on my face into the walls as if
waiting for them to tell me the secret to win back the world
I had lost
I mean

it won't always be like this
I won't always be struggling and our love won't always be lost
inside the pennies of tomorrow's lucky dip
because hope sustains the soul and everything I've ever done
I've done under the influence of dreams
like that night when I whispered into your sleeping ear
that life isn't always about following your heart
and not everyone we meet is good in a world where love
is the only war we've yet to wage

and just then, at that point
I think I fell asleep inside you
because you smiled with those unturned eyes
like all things that have ever been loved smile
and I closed the lights holding your hand
in mine hoping that somehow I could take it with me
when I pass so as to have it build the heaven I would
sleep in forever
I mean

I know I'm not an easy man to be with
and I know I'm hard in places where other men are easy
and I'm quiet when really I should be loud like at a party
where everyone looks like an emancipated photograph
and handshakes are strong and plenty
along with the, 'how you doing?'
'What you working as now and have you gained weight?'
I mean

I've tried it all
I've been that guy at 3am talking circles with the last drunk
trying to help him find his addiction's weary purpose,
and I've stood with empty vodka bottles
waiting in their glass for a lost bus that gave up on its route.
I've spoken with ignorance, I've got angry at the injustices
I have read until my mind has become a blister
filled with all the world's poison
yet when the politics gets too much
and the racism tests my faith in humanity I lean back into myself
and I say
see everything as art, hear everything as music
and feel everything as love
I mean

when I come through the door
like a bitter draft
that fell out the back of winter's long coat
and I see you standing there with a benevolence common
only in things without a self
then I finally start to understand what I mean,
falling asleep inside the streams of your hair
I breathe the ocean again,
I feel my heart beat and sway to the music of an orchestra
conducted by peace
and I remember my name.

I mean
I could write forever, but most of my words
fall on water
I mean.

To Be
Lonely

Always

loneliness
is a troubled conversation
I have with myself
resulting
in one of us

always

leaving

A Difficult Place To Be Human

Non-Believer

I asked her
if she would ever lie to me,
if she would ever leave me,
if she'd ever before woken up
with a winter street chasing summer in her stomach

and she asked me if I believed in God

                                        no was my answer

no was hers

                                I don't believe you I said

we all need to believe in something
my love
            and for a moment I considered it.

She lay her head on my chest
soothing that part of my face that seemed
the most different from hers

I would never hurt you
her palms opened to say

I
swear to God.

Impotent
Man

watering
plants

the closest
a man
can
ever get

to giving
birth.

A Difficult Place To Be Human

Counterpart

one

       more

          time
I get to understand my body
as it lays still against yours
beside yours   above yours
          beneath yours
because my body is a stranger I frown upon
after a lone shower
until like love you appear to touch it
in places that have lived dead and foreign
then as if by the clap of magic
I become filled with movement
and spirited recognition until that moment
when you softly sweep back

removing me

from
myself

one

       more

          time

Empty
Wind

The home is ready. Dainty ornaments
stand supported by their quietude. Scattered books
reveal their authors' lonely secrets.
The music of time surrendering to incandescent
moments that flutter between each warm insect.
My hands are clean. Tonight's food perfumes the
body of each room. The sky lowers itself by night
and I wait your return

to praise all I made. To notice the space
in your wardrobe where your clothes can hang again
like victory flags or ripe fruit or lost birds.
To feel each long hour whisper its devotion to us.
Outside, see how neat the grass looks
like a jealous heart stretching itself upon the earth's
weary back

back to myself. Old violins, low-lights, silent gardens
and leftovers that make for slow eating.
A dog barks at a fence, a dripping tap finds nothing
to clean, the sequential disaster of the neighbours
results again in violent love making and your unseen voice happens
to assure me that there is still a world out there

waiting to be forgotten.

Surgery

Dr. Ahmed said
that he loathed poetry,
removing his surgical mask
from a face that had been awake
since 5am

he said he didn't see its purpose
rinsing his hands under a warm tap
so as to put on a fresh gown
and do it all over again

to make his way back into pain,
into the tumors, the diseases,
the ailments that burn at
the lives of hapless strangers:
to lend his God to their healing.

The theatre lights beamed,
his audience cloaked in sedation
waiting to feel the touch
of his poetry again.

Builder Among Us

Nothing holds. Wide time.
Daylight groans. Rain
pushes. A dusty voice.
Downstairs. Outside. Close by. An engine
rumbles. Another day. Birds and drills.
Moan.
Blue bones. Roll over. Five more minutes.
The toaster's fed. The kettle's bloated.
Keys: the instruments of rushing hands.
We move. Into the standstill.
The industry of life.
Breaking
under the architecture of cemented grind.
The baby-light aches. Same morning. Topless fag smoke.
Sawdust cough. Strong tea. Fuck.
Animal clock purrs.

I leave my eyes

in deep respiration

and kiss one more brick.

The Blind
Beggar's

Grave

A man living blind nudged me properly
to assure me he was there

I turned round to see the skull of the world
buried between both his eyes;
a face that expanded like some waterless rice field -
his body an oil stain.

Holding his hands out like graves
I peered into their progressing earth
looking for the suffering
language was unable to confirm

then suddenly, in that moment,
unfragranced as the atheistic moon
I felt his breath beg for some small life
and yet here I was so full of it

of vision, of talk, of wild dreams
and fresh blood
but I lacked the simple courage to look an old blind man
straight in the palm

muttering to himself
I sat frozen inside the blackness
only he knew how to pilot his way out
from

until I let an old note float down to rescue him
and in return he kept open the grave

where I would break into a thousand pieces of shame.

The
Science
Borrowed

From

Stars

It began,
we began,
with centuries
of fresh cut water,
of open sky,
sun-light painting the wooden deck
where our toes would be still
to be loved;
flowers, plenty flowers
that sprayed the yellow room
with a universe of low aromas,
new days proposed
to each other,
alive with insomnia,
delicate as birth,
leaping forward with high pitched ideas
we rolled like bits from another earth
growing in each others laughter,
sinking in each others slumber
we lived only to throw darts at time

Everything was adventure
Nothing knew how to age

All days gathered
To see what would come next

It was the dream reworked
It was the long hour coming home

We couldn't lose
for loving was winning
and games were what happy children
played best;
we would walk arm in arm

sun in moon
catching the sighs
of the unfulfilled,
the arguments of the cracked
or rich bachelors
spending loneliness's
commission,
the world held open our eyes
ramming its bitter future into our mouths,
we sailed around the hurricane
clinging to transparency, to air,
the world did not know us
but we knew it
as a wounded dog
that needed death

                              I wrote fast, infuriated as if wronged
                              You listened as a leaf does to its season

The lethal enclosure of solitude
A space frigid with echo

                              I dreamt the antithesis of dream
                              Biting down on reticent bones

The tone of loveliness
began to starve itself
my skin subverted
heavy around the mouth,
I noticed the sky less
the hours shrinking
unspoken in a malady of disdain
visitors left snails by my door,
letters remained unopened,

abandoned words,
terrifying mirrors,
the religion of decay
creeping into closed rooms
and the impetuous void that
murders a home;
I lost myself to the self
I lacked
in a bitterness of endings
that are forever
being born

Your voice like broken water
Your eyes baskets of unearthed sorrow

Strength is
A weak man's forgotten habit

Your lips were old stories
I once told myself

It made no sense
the applause and enquiry
my words being sought to heal
a collection of secrets
shared with strangers
it made no sense
how beginnings start,
how love starts,
how art starts,
by accident
with the science borrowed from
stars
I chased their cosmic miracle

around my study
out into the coiling city
where all anguish coheres
like two pints of suffering
being raised to the same God
drunkenly insane

                              Alone I look for you
                              Alone I find you

You love me
Until you see me

                                    Your body
                              A wound I write to

Deeper became the unreal
two indifferent lovers
harpooned by absence
tormented by the contours of memory,
the smell of damp shirts,
the festering nest of longing
your face changing
insisting on isolation
your walk laden with bags
conquered by thoughts
ominous as prepared death
we speak to each other
through shadows
wash our plates separately
cold water running
leaving the front door unlocked
at night
I scribble I love you

whilst you giggle like a little girl
in your sleep

Madness
This whole planet is founded on madness

In a theatre of tragedy
A forest is ablaze

All that remains in a fire
Are the flames

From the stone of tunnels
I feel the hate you kiss me with
I pick the glass out
from inside my bloody breath
hoping to find a clear reflection
so I can make us up again.
Walking out into the night
the masculine abyss
I search the hospital of dreams
for the shape your body made
when it missed me,
I think of all the other beings
and I invent myself in them
away from the loneliness,
away from the sound of love dying.
In everything I touch
I feel the mountains of your bones
hold me like the arms of the world
when the universe whispers, 'every life
is your child.'
I travel to the summit of your last solstice
parting the troubles and ugly fruits

then I find the best part of a new moon
and I await my turn.
A warm rain falls into my mouth
and the stars begin to drown
I grow into the light
the science borrowed from stars
stars that are only ever born
to carry the burden of the sky.

A Difficult Place To Be Human

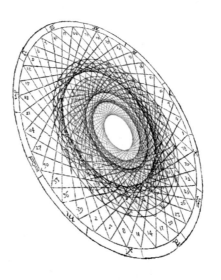

Rain In

Hanoi

Here
alone
in remembering

                        you
I touch
the scar
you made

                        me
to try
heal
the side of you
I know
still
hurts
like I hurt
like rain
hurts
when it

                        falls
on
careless ground

and also
perhaps
because
tonight of all nights
I really
do miss
being
in

                        love
with your

human.

Backpacker

Names, names and streets full of names
they shake hands gripping such sweat,
greeting each other in the language they carry
there on their imperial tongue

and stories, stories full of maneuvers
with death, pestilence,
the shits and how they suffered
            with no women to be their health

to mop the poison away with   Kisses
and the eyelashes of lovely   Heat.
Conversations gambled on blank village ears,
foreign habits that are adopted to try mend

the bleak distances nested in their hearts,
thoughts of a dissipating home at each burning
bend, bamboo chairs to write safety mails
while the gecko hugs completely his precious wall.

The girl from yesterday sobs for the boy
she lost today, gone to the rapidity of the journey,
the ephemeral gulf of restlessness: all is plural she says
asking to be walked to the shack of my own heartache.

(why do the most spectacular roads lead us

                                                nowhere?)

            I write back to the rain

as more arrive. Vagabonds lost in their frenzied bohemia,
hedonists chased by the lustral tassels of utopia,
exhilarated students naive and pathetically groomed
coagulate into familiarity until soon they mutter
where did you come from? Where are you going?

But if there did exist answers to settle such questions
then every backpack would be as weightless as
a snowflake falling around the air of a star

and with that they spill over again. Fly north or gallop south.
A cigarette is left to burn away against itself
on the side of the road. The girl's sobbing stops,
her gardener's hands scattering tracks to some new

                                        destination

that moves further away from her. Gone.
Back into the windy atmosphere of the great voyage,
double-handed or alone following whatever boom
can frighten their hearts into one more shivering miracle

while secretly borrowing each other
to place footsteps on the loneliness
they will spend an entire earth and moon
trying to lose.

A Dinner Candle

And Me

On this night the old dinner candle asked why your chair
happened to be so openly vacant

I could see how alone it supported itself
that halfway lighthouse which would lift both opaque shores

I spoke to its lambency in a voice composed by sorrow
a raucous testimony full of wet wine low down

The more I tried to elucidate your leaving
the more it would flicker and squirm beneath the words

Shrinking wasting that splendid stature we both adored
with each bruised syllable that left my mouth

I could not stop even through the bulbs of burning tears
that rolled down the side of its softening red body

I could not stop as I watched it become an embarrassed mess
with all anguish eating away at such proud form

A struggling glow was all that remained to say you once loved me
and I too had once loved you so thoroughly so unrestricted

A melting face whose tiny ears were at last to be swallowed
by the flame of agony dying to the only story it was unable to bear

And I finished in darkness.

Nha Trang City

Fiery streets
that spit horns
burning midnight inside a nest
of wooden stars.

Bikes meeting each other
at a deadly stop seconds before hitting
the heart of the moon's crying tumor

the amputated seller at the end of my road
everyday, every night, everyday, every night
sends the same question
to my same tired answer

a city living around a broken traffic light,
the old lady chews rice with her gums,
a coconut breaks its belly on the road to bleed
poverty smells of rotting fish
and trampled dragon fruit
then the noise, the noise that grows from
inside the immense bark of survival

little children leap up to my wandering
with crystal skin and pinewood eyes
pointing out in a dialect I can understand
only as taunt;
I write the word grief
on the face of a 100,000 dong note
hoping they will always remember
to play with whatever they make of it.

Passing the squatting mechanics
sparks massacre the air's fragile pupils,
metal makes love to more metal,

a half dog chases the ghost of a famished cat,
a lizard sits on the side of the road
waiting for Buddha to show
and the shirtless peasant pisses
a dead yellow river
whilst vomiting up
all that he wished he could hold
like an organ
within.

All these signs, tokens of metaphysics
peak the nettled quality of my dismay

and again I think of you sweetheart, sitting without me,
drinking a light drink, surrounded by
rich smelling cakes and friends
who make you laugh until the table shakes
and you get the sudden urge to dance
to music I always said lacked soul and
good earth.

I have come away to find you once more
to the pallid throne of memory because
home has left me.

On the night we spoke about suicide
I insisted that there was nothing more dangerous than an ocean
watching a troubled man inhale his own silence,
yes my burden is hostage to a sack of poems
I tremble to read back
overladen with meaning I try to rattle them off
as fiction, as pretend, as plastic,
but none of this holds use, the ocean knows,
for it has seen many strong men
become broken by sand.

This magnificent ocean
-ancient sky of ground-
I can see those green hills
of gypsy glass carry the secrets
placed upon them back into that
deep solicitude, that watery dune,
I can see how the ocean is imperishable,
how in war it can never be
destroyed, dismembered or rearranged,
how lions cower to its roar,
how ships of the sophisticate become
grammar on a page.

I see many things as the surf falls in
with its elated gleam fixed on its silver lips
bequeathed with the blessings of warm saltwater

then I notice that with each strike of wave
the mighty shore only ever moves into the path of its dying
as it lives on shrinking
in its own golden
loneliness.

Dearest
Empathy

As the singular boat of time
carries you further into its water
you learn
that not all people are wicked
that poverty of mind wrecks surer
than poverty of cloth
that love always falls back into love
and that trees too pray
and animals too hurt.
You will see that not everyone
cries with tears
and in places where no light shines
you will always find
the strongest
dark.

Until the day when the body
becomes filled with a million hearts
each working like floating bells
against the deep turn of heavy water.

A Difficult Place To Be Human

The loneliest
people are
those

surrounded
by an
entire city

Anthony Anaxagorou

Web – www.anthonyanaxagorou.com
Email – mail@anthonyanaxagorou.com
Twitter – Anthony1983

Other titles by the author:

Card Not Accepted
Poems to Maya
Pale Remembered
The Lost Definition Of Hope
Let This Be The Call
Returning Stranger
A Sad Dance